S[illegible] YOURSELF LAUGHING

20 OF THE BEST SHIT JOKES

(plus 10 shit cartoons by Rus)

Hopkins Muir

Published by JHJ22 Publishing

Cover by ebookdesign.co.uk

ISBN 978-0-9932518-5-6

What others might be saying about this 5 x 8 toilet roll, SHIT YOURSELF LAUGHING

'Probably the funniest bathroom book I have never read...' (John Lloyd – *The New Financial Times*)

'Such a useful booklet...' (Arson Welles – *The Old York Times*)

'What a load of shite...' (Nicola Surgeon – *The Scotswoman*)

'*Funny as shite...*' (Me – *Glasgow 2018*)

'*Funnier than shite...*' (Him – *Later*)

'Laughter accelerates breathing, raises blood pressure, increases pulse rates, improves ventilation. It can increase adrenalin, which in turn may activate the release of endorphins and enkephalins...' (Howard Jacobson – *Seriously Funny*).

It also helps you shite. So, if nothing else, keep this booklet in the bathroom and open it every time you are... eh... stuck...

CONTENTS

SHIT YOURSELF LAUGHING

PROLEGOMENON: (prefatory matter, as opposed to faecal matter)

SCATOLOGY: 1 (The Concise Oxford Dictionary) study of coprolites; preoccupation with excrement; preoccupation with obscene literature.

COPROPHILIA: 2 (Collins English Dictionary): abnormal interest in faeces and evacuation thereof.

COPRO: (ibid 2): Dung OR obscenity…

OBSCENITY: 3 (Collins SHUGEST EVER Dictionary): the state or art of being obscene.

OBSCENE: (ibid 3): (i) Offensive or outrageous to accepted standards of decency or modesty. (ii) Law: tending to deprave or corrupt. (iii) Disgusting; repellent. From Latin – *obscenus* – 'inauspicious.'

Why should a word derived from the Greek (*kopros*) for dung be equated with

Why the difference? Apart from the scatologically obvious comment that 'The South' has still not learned to do it properly with an extra 'E' for effort right at the end of the process, we don't really ken. Maybe it is slightly more PC to *shit* than to *shite*. (Like saying or even using *ass* instead of *arse*?) Maybe it is a combination of euphemism / bowdlerisation or even snobbery if not elitism. If so, we shall definitely use the *five* letter word from now on… apart from the title that was deliberately aimed at the mass market of shits down South (who are maybe too busy making money to take time to shite properly).

And to end on a serious if not frivolous note… forget, for a wee while at least, *memento mori*, and where we are all going. This is a reminder about where we ALL came from, and to a largish or smallerish extent, to what we shall all return.

'If comedy, in all its changing shapes, has one overriding preoccupation, it is this: that we resemble beasts more closely than we

obscenity? Victorian values or what? We all defecate. (Well most of us.)

So does calling it shit or shite make it obscene? Some would say yes, and label it coprolalia.

COPROLALIA: (ibid 2): Obsessive use of obscene or foul language.

We say bollocks or even shite to all of that. If a joke is funny, it is funny, and that is as analytical or philosophical as we shall nearly be.

So all these jokes are about shite (hopefully none are shite jokes). So why are they exclusively about shite? Mainly because we liked the title – *Shit Yourself Laughing*. But also, once we put our minds to it, we unearthed (often remembered) 20 crackers…

Linguistic Note: (not philosophical but empirical) The Celtic Fringe (Scotland, Ireland, maybe Wales even?) plus the North of England SHITE. The rest of our sceptred, if not scented, isle would appear to SHIT.

resemble gods, and that we make great fools of ourselves the moment we forget it.'

Howard Jacobson – *Seriously Funny*

ENJOY.

Chapter 1

BETTER TIMES

A man returns to Glasgow after 50 years in the States. After a city-centre shopping spree, during which he has a couple of pints, he is caught short and only just makes it to the nearest men's public toilet. In mid-stream, he is astonished when he recognises an old friend of his, who appears to have the job of keeping the public convenience tidy.

They enter into a typical Glaswegian conversation.

'Is that yourself?' the man asks his friend.

'It is, aye.'

'After all these years,' the man says. 'I cannae believe it. So what're you up to these days?'

'Keeping this place clean. What does it look like?'

ADOLESCENT DOGS

Chapter 2

THIS IS MINCE

In an elevator in a high-rise building, a social worker is about to light up a fag on his way down after a home visit to a poor lonely soul on one of the upper floors. Before reaching the ground floor, the lift stops, and a punter gets in – your typical Glasgow short-arse, and someone the social worker has never seen before – who starts talking to him in that friends-with-everyone manner peculiar to the people of Glasgow.

'Ah, fuck it,' the wee man says, distressed. 'This place is going down the fucking drain. Goin from bad tae fucking worse, so it is, ah'm tellin ye…'

The social worker hides his fag, and gives a grim smile in response.

The wee man looks up at him, as if appealing to his sense of fairness. 'Ma flat's just been broken into. Bastarts stole all ma CDs. Ripped ma sofa to buggery. Smashed ma kitchen to fuck.' The wee man shakes his head in disgust. 'And they even took ma pot of mince aff the stove and done a shite in it.'

Just then, the lift stops at the ground floor. As the door opens, the wee man steps into the lobby, and says, 'I had to throw half of it oot!'

Chapter 3

LEARNING ON THE JOB

A Glasgow sewer worker has spent the last 50 years down in the drains. Glasgow's Lord Provost feels this sterling (pre-Brexit) service should be rewarded, so he and his hangers-on decide the gold watch should be presented in situ.

They duly find the appositely proximate person-hole cover and descend into chthonian stygian gloom to be met by a surprisingly chirpy sewer worker singing away and working his various miracles with the river of turds that are forever floating past.

'Tell me Mr Smith…'

'Call me Shug, please, Mister Lord Provost.'

'Shug, before I present you with this token of our esteem for your 50 years working alone down here, I have to ask… well to be blunt, what do you do to maintain your interest in all this… er… shite?'

'Aye, there's plenty of shite, but there's plenty to keep me interested. More than that, my Lord… very educational this job, so it is. For instance, you know I could be a detective by now, the things I've learned down here… for instance, see that shite going by right now, surrounded by the wood shavings, that was done by a joiner. And see this next one coming along, aye the one with all the curly hair sticking to it - that once belonged to a barber… oh, and yes, the one emerging right now… that is definitely ma wife's…'

'Come now, Shug, how on earth could you know?'

'It's got ma sandwiches tied to it.'

IS THAT CHOCOLATE
OR IS IT SHITE?

MUNCH... MUNCH...
... OH... IT'S SHITE

JUST AS WELL I
DIDN'T STEP ON IT

Chapter 4

BLACK JAKE

Tenderfoot stupidly gets lost in the Badlands. Suddenly, from behind a rock appears a huge evil looking cowboy brandishing two six shooters who demands, 'Get off yer horse, pilgrim!'

Tenderfoot obliges.

'Take off yer duds, pilgrim!'

Tenderfoot protests but is informed, 'I am Black Jake, pilgrim, the meanest, evillest, baddest bad ass this side of the cotton pickin Pecos, and what Black Jake asks, Black Jake gets. Strip, pilgrim!!'

Tenderfoot duly obliges.

'Pish, pilgrim!!'

Tenderfoot protests:

'But, I've just been—'

‘Ah sayed PISH!’

Somehow Tenderfoot manages to create a smallish puddle.

‘Shit, pilgrim. SHIT!!’

‘Oh, I mean to say… I have a problem in that department… not too regular…’

‘Black Jake says SHIIIIIT!!!’

This, plus a bullet whizzing past the Tenderfoot’s skull seems to do the trick and a respectable sized shite is deposited atop the rapidly evaporating puddle.

‘Now EAT it, pilgrim!’

‘Now that’s not—’

‘EAT THE FUCKER!!!!’ is accompanied by two bullets knocking off the Tenderfoot’s new Stetson.

Tenderfoot obliges. Black Jake steals his horse and leaves the Tenderfoot stranded in the middle of the Badlands.

Some hours later a dishevelled wreck of a Tenderfoot staggers into the saloon in the nearest town and demands a half pint shandy to slake his raging thirst.

The barman laughs and suggests that the tenderfoot looks as if he has walked all the way through the Badlands.

'I have,' replies the Tenderfoot.

Barman laughs incredulously and says, 'You'll be telling me next that you met Black Jake…'

'I did.'

'Absolute Hogwash! NOBODY meets Black Jake and lives to tell the tale. My friend, You DO… NOT… KNOW Black Jake—'

'Know him?!… I've just had lunch with him!'

Chapter 5

THE JOHNSON BROTHERS

As legend has it, the Johnson brothers were the world's worst singing act. And because of that, they had not worked for nearly twenty years when one day their agent phones them out of the blue with the offer of a gig in London. They are thrilled, but he warns them, 'It doesn't pay much, so to keep expenses down, I've arranged for you to travel by barge for free.'

They duly board the barge and are directed to a tiny cabin just under the deck. The barge starts off but very soon stops and the Johnson brothers hear the following conversation above deck:

LOCKMASTER: 'Bargemaster! State your cargo!!'

BARGEMASTER: 'Lockmaster, I carry 300 thousand litres of shite… and the Johnson brothers.'

Every ten minutes the barge stops as it and its cargo travel through the series of locks… '300,000 litres of shite… and the Johnson brothers,' is repeated more or less ad nauseam, when suddenly the hatch is flung open and the Bargemaster sees a hand furiously fluttering a five pound note accompanied by the voices of the Johnson brothers for once bizarrely in unison and harmony, pleading:

'Mr Bargemaster, please sir, before we get to London… just one time… any chance of us *topping* the bill?'

'Henry! We have a perfectly good bathroom inside, and what's more, the Tate Gallery won't be interested in that sort of shit.'

Chapter 6

SHITE FLYING LESSON

A guy goes up for his first flying lesson. He is nervous despite the instructor assuring him that in the case of any emergency he would take over via the dual controls. Things go well. The guy is loving it, when suddenly the instructor has a heart attack and snuffs it.

The guy immediately panics but somehow while battering all the controls he manages to make contact with Glasgow Airport's Air Traffic Control.

'Fucks sake do something!' the guy screams.

'Do not panic, sir, we shall talk you down, sir—'

'Panic! Fucking panic! You would panic too if you were flying upside fucking down.'

‘Calm down sir, we know this is your first lesson, I mean to say how do you know, sir, you are actually flying upside down?

‘Cos the shite’s coming oot ma collar!’

Chapter 7

RED HOT POKER

Man goes to the doctor and says, 'Doctor, the strangest thing… for this last month I have lost control of my bowels… in simple language I shite myself at least twice a day. Like on the way here for instance.'

Doctor interrupts and says, 'Nothing strange about that. Quite common. There's a lot of it going about… but let me examine you. Drop your trousers.'

Man obliges and says, 'But you don't understand, the strange thing is my shites no longer smell.'

Doctor quickly produces a red hot poker from his red hot poker cupboard and approaches the man who screams, 'Doctor! You're surely not going to stick that thing up my arse.'

'Certainly not… your bowel motion has an extremely pungent vile smell… I'm going to stick this up your nose!'

MM.. WONDERFUL JOB THOUGH YOUR HUSBAND HAS MADE OF IT... IT'S NOT QUITE WHAT WE WERE LOOKING FOR

Chapter 8

NO LONGER

Guy goes into a bar and asks for a pint. As the barman pours, the man drops his breeks and deposits one big long shite on the floor. Barman is outraged.

The guy cringes and profusely apologises. ‘I’m sorry. I’m so sorry… I’m really EMBARRASSED.’

Next week same guy comes in and Barman tells him he is barred but the guy protests, ‘It’s okay I’m cured.’

Barman relents and starts pouring the pint but the same thing happens again – a large shite is plopped onto the floor.

Guy breaks down and says, ‘I’m sorry. I’m so sorry… and I’m really *really* EMBARRASSED.’

Barman chucks him (and his shite) out into the street.

Next week same guy comes in.

Barman orders him out.

Guy protests, 'But I REALLY am cured now. Honest. Right hand up to God…'

Despite himself Barman starts pouring a pint only to witness another monster shite thudding onto his floor.

'Ya filthy wee bastard! Ye swore ye were cured.'

'But I am,' says the wee guy grinning broadly. 'I'm *no longer* EMBARRASSED.'

Chapter 9

LONG NECK

A Blackpool landlady is returning with her late morning shopping to be met on her front steps by a large hoity-toity lady who had just checked in for the first time earlier that same morning. The woman is obviously outraged and bumps her large suitcase down the steep steps and shouts *en passant* at her erstwhile landlady:

'Dreadful establishment. Awful. Worst ever.'

Landlady hurt, demands, 'What do you mean?'

'There is no toilet paper in your communal bathroom! Absolutely disgraceful!'

Landlady, relieved that's all it is, matter of factly says, 'Well, my dear, you have a tongue in your head.'

Lady says, 'But one doesn't have a neck like a bloody giraffe!'

NO PAPER AGAIN? OH WELL, AT LEAST I'M WEARING MY BROWN TROUSERS!
Rus.

Chapter 10

A Wee Limerick

There was a young lady called Alice,

Who shat in the Vatican Palace.

Twasn't physical need

That triggered her deed,

But sheer bloody Protestant malice.

Chapter 11

TWO TENNERS

Guy gets a bollocking from wife BEFORE a boy's night out with his pal.

'Your last warning,' she says. 'You come home once more the least bit worse for wear and we're finished!'

Guy promises faithfully to behave. Unlike ALL the other times.

Usual happens and he gets blootered and is suddenly, violently sick down his best (one and only) suit.

'Aw fuck. What am I gonnie do?'

'No problem, says his equally drunk pal. 'Here's a tenner. Tell your wife that some drunk did it all over you and show her this £10 he gave you for the cleaners bill. Here take it. AND KEEP IT IN YOUR HAND TO SHOW HER, ya mug!'

Guy eventually gets home to be met with wife and her wrath at the front door. As she starts to lose it he waves the tenner in her face and explains using his pal's ruse about some drunk vomiting all down the front of his best suit. 'See… look. He gave me ten quid to pay to clean it up…'

'Okay…,' she reluctantly says. 'But what's the other ten pounds for in your other hand?'

'Oh, that's from the nice guy who shat in my trousers…'

BLACK PLAGUE?!

NA... JUST THE SKITS

Rus

Chapter 12

SINGING THROUGH IT

A down-at-heels agent somehow discovers a unique talent… a man who can really sing through his arse. The agent puts him to the test and discovers that this bloke is not only a good singer, with a range from poshest Classic to prosaic Pop, but every piece is delivered, if not rendered, through his arse.

The agent has great difficulty in persuading the sphincter-singer that his talent is not only unique, but is extremely exploitable, and could turn him into a global superstar. He eventually manages to talk him into performing at the London Palladium. The sphincter-songster reluctantly agrees on one condition: his face is never to be shown – only his arse.

After weeks of expensive, extensive publicity and hype, and fine-trimming of the singer's arse hairs, and applying lashings of *Clearasil* to the plethora of spots surrounding them, the evening duly arrives.

The theatre is sold out, and as the band strikes up, the curtains part ever so slightly and an arse emerges.

Then all of a sudden it dumps a huge shite onto the stage. ‘Sorry,’ it says. ‘Just clearing my throat.’

Chapter 13

OPTICAL ILLUSION

Guy bursts into an opticians carrying a violin case.

The optician asks, ‘Can I help you, sir?’

The guy says, ‘I bloody hope so,’ and opens the violin case.

Inside is a huge shite that takes up the whole case.

The optician is outraged and roars, ‘How dare you!!! How dare you sully my premises with… with… THAT!!! It’s a doctor you need. Or a bloody psychiatrist.’

The guy interrupts, and says, ‘No, no, you don’t understand. Every time I do one of them, my eyes water.’

I'D GET OUT BEFORE HE STARTS – IT'S THE WORST SHIT YOU'VE EVER HEARD.

Chapter 14

WHY ME?

A wee horrible looking perpetually moaning whinger believes he is having an even worse day than his normal awful ones. Everything seems to have gone wrong. He ripped his trousers on dressing, burned the toast, the lavvy wouldn't flush, and when the TV blew up, he bursts out his front door, waves his fist up to the sky to demand:

'Why me?!!!'

Instantly the clouds part, an enormous foot descends and crushes the moaning whinger and explains:

'Cos yer a wee shite!'

Chapter 15

NOT A PRESCRIPTION

Guy staggers into the doctor with a bulging sack over his shoulder, hoists sack onto GP's desk and gasps, 'Doctor, you have to help me…'

The doctor opens the sack and staggers back holding his breath and sinks into his swivel chair, almost passing out as the guy speaks again:

'For the last two months I've been dumping one of those monsters six times a day. It's hellish embarrassing. I often get caught short and have nowhere to…' He stops when he see the Doctor reaching for a pen. 'Here, what's that you're writing? Is that a prescription?

'No. It's a licence to shite in the street.'

MY MUM'S NOT SHAT FOR TWO MONTHS!

SHE LOOKS OKAY TO ME

OH RIGHT, I SEE WHAT YOU MEAN

Chapter 16

ULTIMATE CHAT UP LINE

An adolescent male has an unrequited passion for the girl next door. Every morning he watches her head down the back garden to the outside toilet. He desperately wants to win her, but is chronically shy and hopelessly tongue-tied.

He seeks his pal's advice. This Lothario tells him, 'Bump into her accidentally on purpose when she's coming back from her 'ablutions' – she'll be at her most comfortable and receptive then.'

'But what will I say to her?' asks Master Shy.

'The first thing that comes into your head. Be natural. Be yourself. Women love that. They hate nervousness. It makes them nervous. Just bloody talk to her. Tomorrow!'

Next evening Lothario is met by a crestfallen Master Shy.

‘Well, did you talk to her?’

‘Uh huh.’

‘On her way back from the outside Kazzy?’

‘Yes.’

‘Well, what did you say?’

‘Enjoy your shite, then?’

Chapter 17

CROFTER'S ORIGINAL

Old crofter in remote highlands wins the regional sheep-dog trials every year. The prize is a week at the London Ritz. Not having hot or even cold running water in his croft, he has never been privy to any privies. So first time at the Ritz, he shites (and pishes) behind the hotel bedroom curtains for the week.

Despite not receiving any complaints, the second year he wins the trials, he has second thoughts about where to shite, so decides to slide his shites under the bed. The next year, the third time, he decides to deposit his shites in the wardrobe.

By this time his dog is so renowned that he enters it for The Nationals. It wins and the prize is not only a fortnight in the Ritz but also £5,000.

His pals talk him into installing a WC in his home.

So back in the Ritz, he now knows what that funny wee room and the funny wee thingumajig is used for and consequently does his business accordingly.

He returns to his croft to be met by a telegram that states:

'Okay, ya old bastard. You win. We give up. Where the fuck have you hidden the fuckers this time?!

THE TRUTH ABOUT NOAH

Chapter 18

THE OLD FIRMISH

A very drunk Glasgow Rangers supporter enters the Celtic end of the terracing at an Old Firm match. BIG mistake.

He realises his error too late. He is squashed and surrounded by Celtic supporters. He quickly receives a batter on the shoulder and an instruction:

'Get us two *Bovrils* ya blue-nosed c***!… And leave wan o' yer shoes.'

Discretion being the better part of 'a doing,' Rangers fan duly obliges, returns, passes over the two *Bovrils* and puts his shoe back on to a squelch and the concomitant discovery of a fresh shite in the aforesaid shoe.

Later Rangers score and our man receives the immediate demand for, 'Another two *Bovrils* ya Proddy orange bastard, now! And leave yer other shoe…'

Rangers fan returns and delivers two cups of *Bovril* only to find a shite in his other shoe. Before the end of the game, he decides to leave early, in case Rangers score again. He somehow manages to double squelch his way out of the ground without further mishap.

Outside the ground he is met by a TV outside broadcast unit that is capturing Vox Pops about Sectarianism, Bigotry and Violence in Scottish Football.

Our Rangers fan squelches across and grabs the microphone to bark, 'There will never be an end to violence and religious bigotry! Not until these bastards stop shiting in our shoes, and we stop pishing in their *Bovril*!'

Chapter 19

WITH ENEMAS LIKE THESE

Disgruntled guy barges into his GP's surgery.

'What's wrong Mr Archer, you seem upset?'

'Call yourself a doctor? See these enemas you gave me for my chronic constipation?'

'Yes, I do remember.'

'Well I've been taking them for three weeks now, and for all the good they've done me, I would have been as well sticking them up my arse!'

GREAT HUNTER ... GREAT
LOSS ... BUT SHAT ON
BY A BRONTISOREARSE

Chapter 20

VLADIMIR & ESTRAGON

{With NO apology to Sammy Beckett}

Beckett's two tramps, Vladimir & Estragon, are on the park bench waiting for Godot. Suddenly, Vladimir sniffs the air, then turns to Estragon and declares, 'Estragon, thou filthy cunt, thou've shattest thineself again, haven't thou?!'

'Fuck off ya poof! I'll have thou know I have not shatteth myself.'

'Yes you have thou filthy fucking bastard…'

'I haveth not!'

'Remove thine trousers and let one inspect forthwith.'

'With the greatest of pleasure.'

Estragon's voluminous trousers are removed to reveal layer upon layer of shite all around his nether regions.

Vladimir exclaims, 'I knewest it! There you are thou cunt, verily thou art covered in layers of fucking shite thou dirty filthy lying bastard. How can thou claim to NOT having shat thyself?!!'

'Dearest Vladimir, I thoughtest thou meant *today*.'

AUTHORS' NOTE

Both Ian and Frank acknowledge with much appreciation and gratitude the tireless effort and surprising patience of the cartoonist, Russell Campbell, without whom this joke booklet would have been... well... it would have been more (or less) shite!!

Russell has written for Scotland's leading quality newspapers, *The Herald* and *The Scotsman*, and also contributed to the (Glasgow) *Evening Times*. Russell has been a joke writer for the greeting card industry, with over two million cards sold bearing his jokes, including work for *Hallmark USA*. As a cartoonist, over a thousand of his cartoons have appeared in leading newspapers and business publications.

Russell is also the author of three books. *Movers and Shirkers* (2014) a novel based on insider trading and is set in London. *Fool Me Fool You* (2014) is a novel about deception within an Edinburgh bank. And *Bunches of Grapes* (2010) is a collection of original bagpipe music.

ABOUT THE AUTHORS

Ian Hopkins:

Contracted (and paid!)
SERIOUS COMEDY WRITING of Ian Hopkins.

NOVELS: (both serious comic, putatively satiric)

1) *Skelp the Aged* (with John Duignan) – April 2016.

2) *The Buick Stops Here* (with John Duignan) – October 2017.

STAGE:

1) *Citizen Singh* (with Gurmeet Mattu).

2) *Albatross Soup* (with John Duignan).

3) *Every Bloody Sunday* (with Gurmeet Mattu).

TELEVISION:

1) Not The Nine O Clock News.

2) Three of a Kind.

3) Naked Video.

4) Spitting Image.

RADIO:

1) Naked Radio.

2) Six of the Best.

More info on Ian can be seen on *Facebook* under '*Skelp the Aged*'.

Frank Muir:

Born far too many years ago in Glasgow, Scotland, Frank graduated from Strathclyde University, Glasgow, with a degree he hated. He assures everyone who cares to listen, that he never wanted to be a civil engineer, but with youthful apathy found himself working in Glasgow's Department of Architecture and Related Services designing..? you got it… sewerage schemes, and wondering what he wanted to do with his life. Working overseas sounded like a good idea, so off he went to the Middle East – Saudi Arabia, Qatar, Bahrain – then the

USA, where he worked and lived for over 20 years, regrettably as a civil engineer.

But living and working overseas helped Frank appreciate the raw beauty of his home country, and his love of reading fiction helped him understand that his true calling was to be a crime novelist. For information on his novels, visit www.frankmuir.com

Printed in Great Britain
by Amazon